MW01228685

This book belongs to the brand of:

Beautifully Branded

THE GIRL'S GUIDE TO PERSONAL BRANDING & UNDERSTANDING THE ANATOMY OF BRAND YOU

OLIVIA OMEGA

Illustrated by M.J. Logan

ISBN-10: 1544113153
ISBN-13: 978-1544113159

www.OliviaOmega.com

Books may be purchased in quantity and/or special sales by contacting the publisher at the information below.

Wallace Marketing Group
200 Quebec St., Bldg. 300 Suite 111
Denver, CO 80230
info@wallacemarketinggroup.com

Cover & Interior Design by: Olivia Omega Wallace
Illustrations by: M.J. Logan
Cover Photo by: Lindsay Glatz
10 9 8 7 6 5 4 3 2
First Printed 2015
Printed in USA

Dedication

To the two ladies that have influenced my life beyond words. My mom whose unfailing love and support has been monumental in becoming the woman I am today. And my daughter who's unique spirit and beautiful outlook on life has inspired me to always look on the bright side, be proud of my work and push to complete this incredible project.

Table of Contents

Acknowledgements

Thank you to my Lord and Savior Jesus Christ to whom I owe my life and every accomplishment. Thank you to all those who encouraged me to write this book... repeatedly, and those that continued to encourage me until it was complete. Thank you to my Pastors for their support and spiritual guidance. Thank you to all of the amazing women entrepreneurs that have crossed my path over the years and who remind me daily that this is what I was put on this earth to do. Thank you to my illustrator/doodler and task master, my daughter Malia, for continuing to push me and asked me daily for a full year if I've finished my book yet.

Lastly, thank you to my fears. The completion of the initial version of this book was put off for well over a year because I was worried about the opinions of others and I was afraid that it might not turn out as great as I envisioned it, and that it wouldn't be good enough. Finally publishing this book has been one of the most vulnerable things I have ever done. It has allowed me to overcome my fears, embrace my imperfections and further step into my God-given purpose.

"He has made everything ***beautiful*** for its own time."
– Ecclesiastes 3:11

"And I will make of the a great nation, and I will bless thee, and make your ***name*** great; and thou shalt be a blessing."
– Genesis 12:2

Chapter One

Jane of All Trades

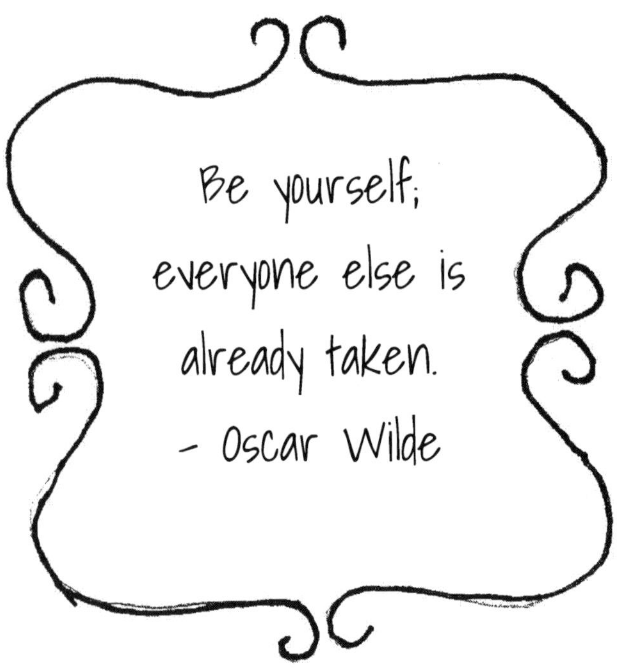
Be yourself;
everyone else is
already taken.
- Oscar Wilde

Jane of all trades. She may be popular, but she isn't very happy.

I've always been pretty good at most everything I've tried in life. This is both a major blessing and a curse. My senior year in high school I was named "Renaissance Woman" for being well-rounded and talented in so many areas. And when I graduated from college, the Business School honored me with the Leadership Award. This was the beginning of a slew of accomplishments as well as the birth of my battle with procrastination. The struggle was real simply because I learned that I could put off a project, paper, speech, presentation, you name it until the last minute and then kill it. I would blow things out of the water with little preparation. This is a wonderful skill when it is absolutely necessary to step into a situation that is completely unexpected. Like being asked on the spot to address a crowd of several thousand people in a football stadium...true story. But it is a flaw that can be detrimental to success.

Well, college was quite some time ago and with age comes the inability to effectively pull off consecutive all-nighters with ease. Add marriage, two kids, divorce, life's wear and tear, another marriage (I know I don't look old enough, but remember I'm an overachiever) and it gets increasingly harder to just wing it and win. This is where I will fully admit that procrastination is a problem.

Furthermore, the blessing and curse of being pretty good at many things was that I often found myself in situations because I was the best fit or the most logical choice in the room. After all, I'm a Renaissance Woman. It makes sense. While I could fill pages with examples of this, I will highlight two, both pertaining to my athletic career (this is where people who know me should laugh out loud). I'm a dancer. I love to dance and probably have been doing so since I could walk. This is where I can definitely say my daughter is my child. My son is also definitely my child for that matter. Dance parties have become a ritual in our family so much so that I have a disco ball hanging in the dining room. It's used so much that I have a spare in the basement just in case of an emergency. So instead of doing sports when I entered high school, I danced.

Senior year I decided to flip the script and try out for track and cheerleading. In track I started running short distances, but wasn't entirely fast enough (I didn't suck, but I wasn't amazing by any means). My mediocre skills landed me on the JV team...ouch. But when there weren't many girls brave enough to wrestle the hurdles (and I literally mean wrestle...I still have the scars to prove it), I was moved up to Varsity – by default. Even in my rare higher than average mediocrity, I would somehow end up being the best for the job.

In both high school and college I tried out for the cheerleading team my Freshmen years. I didn't make it either time. Talk about a déjà vu moment. But I went back a couple years later both times, tried out again and made both teams. Yay! But my tumbling skills were lacking. They weren't nonexistent, but admittedly below mediocre. Let's not forget about my amazing leadership skills and accomplishments. And you can't have a cheerleader without a leader right? So guess who was co-captain in college? Again, the best for the job description despite my crappy back handspring and non-existent standing back tuck.

Fast forward 20 years to present day. I've now defined not only who I am, but who I want to be. Which really didn't begin to happen until my early thirties, so for those of you in your twenties, don't rush the process. I've narrowed in on not just branding, but personal branding as my focus and expertise. And not just for anyone, but for creative women entrepreneurs. And now I've written this book on the topic. If there is one single thing I've learned since high school, it's that the title of Renaissance Woman didn't serve me. It actually set me up for failure.

I call it “renaissance woman syndrome”. I was praised for being creative and skilled in so many areas. That started to be the definition of my self worth. If you need something, most likely, I’m your girl. You need something made, call Olivia. You need a photographer, ask Olivia. You need a logo designed (I think I was hired to make my first one in high school), call Olivia. You need wedding invitations, Olivia would be perfect. You need someone to hem your pants, Olivia can do that. You need a website, Olivia does that. I felt (and honestly still find myself working to balance) the need to be all things to everyone. Not because I felt I had to, but because I could. When you have the ability to do all the things why not do them? I have the skill and I’m pretty good at it, so why not? Plus I’m a giver and I can’t help it.

Entrepreneurship, marriage, motherhood, womanhood and sisterhood are all rich habitats that feed the giver trait. Sometimes to a point where it can take control and take over a person’s livelihood. If you are all five like me, a woman, entrepreneur, sister, mother and wife, self-awareness and self-care are critical to achieving balance and happiness. I’m not talking about the bubble bath, glass of wine type of self care. But the saying no, delegating, setting healthy boundaries and putting your feelings first type of self love. I stink at this which is why I’ll never write a book on this topic!

The renaissance woman effect will burn you out quicker than any job, rendering you physically, emotionally and mentally drained. Trust me! This is coming from a pro...and recovering renaissance woman.

When I'm hired as a consultant for a big brand or corporation, they usually seek me out for a very specific purpose – usually to rebrand their company or to establish a social media strategy. The need is focused and so I come alongside the company's team members who are each honed in on their specific role within that team.

On the flip side, when I work with entrepreneurs or creative coaches and consultants who are just starting out or who are a bit more established, but still need to evaluate everything about their brand and business, they need pretty much everything! And they can't afford an entire team of people working to help establish their brand. In this case, my renaissance woman pops her head up with her multiple hats and I think to myself "I can do that! I can do ALL of that!" From brand and growth strategy, brand identity, product creation, design work, website development, social media, photography and more. Phew! I can do all of those things pretty well. Better than your average Jane. But that doesn't mean I should. And it definitely doesn't mean I can execute on all of those things well.

It's challenging because my heart and true passion is working with women entrepreneurs and nothing gives me more joy than to see them take a dream or idea and make it come to life. But I also know that as I attempt to do everything, I simply cannot do it all well. I often tell my potential and current clients to steer clear of those who position themselves as a "jack of all trades". As an entrepreneur and consultant, I have to resist doing this all of the time. Trust me, I know it's tempting!

One of the greatest pieces of advice I've received is that your gifts and talents are not necessarily your purpose. And just because you can doesn't mean you should. We'll talk about it more later, but doing a deep dive into who you are, what you have to offer and the difference between what you are able to do and what you were put on this earth to do is one of the most important elements to building your brand. It's the first step – examining the heart. At the core of who you are as a person and as a woman lies your unique purpose.

Your gifts and talents are not necessarily your purpose. Just because you can doesn't mean you should.

#beautifullybranded #purpose
@oliviaomega

The premises of this entire book and the concept of "beautifully branded" is that when you are authentically yourself, leveraging your unique talents, charm and personality (and yes, all of your many flaws), you have no competition because there is no other you. Even identical twins, which are the closest any two people can get to each other by sharing the same DNA, still have differences that make them unique. What separates you from everyone else in your profession, field, industry and community is you. And your success depends on your ability to market your uniqueness in a way that is authentic and valuable to your target audience.

If you take away just one thing from this book it is this:

When you are authentically yourself,
Your brand has no competition.

#beautifullybranded #personalbranding #beyou
@oliviaomega

What are my talents/gifts vs. my purpose?

Chapter Two

Your Branding Handbook

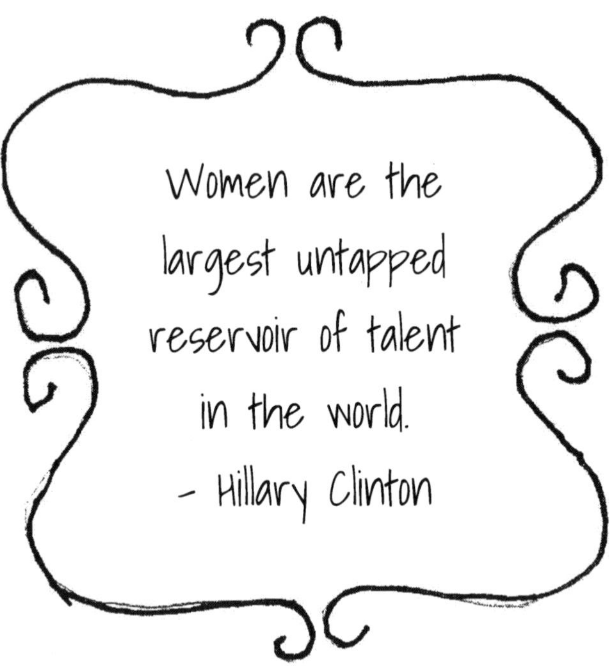
Women are the
largest untapped
reservoir of talent
in the world.
- Hillary Clinton

How to get the most out of this handbook/workbook...

This isn't a text book filled with branding and marketing definitions. It's not an exhaustive must-do list of best practices. And it definitely isn't an end-all and be-all. It truly is a guide book with stories and advice from my heart to yours that convey overarching strategies and tactics to establish your name and build your expertise. It's not meant to be read just once, but to be referenced and written on.

Break out your favorite pens and colored pencils ladies!

I have a confession to make. I absolutely love pretty journals! I collect them (too many to count), but I have a hard time writing in them. I simply don't want to mess them up. They are so beautiful! But this book is meant for just that – to be messed up, highlighted, written on, crossed out, scribbled in and doodled on. And if you haven't already done so, make sure to write your name on the first page to break it in!

It's also intentionally this perfect cute little pocket size so you can take it with you anywhere and everywhere. Once completed, it will be your brand's bible, reminding you of what you stand for and who you serve.

IMPORTANT NOTE: Available resources, tactics and ways to execute on you brand strategy change and improve daily. I'm sure Facebook has updated their business page features and ad functionality at least 25 times since I initially began the process of publishing this book. Because of the rapidly changing nature of the world we live in, you will find that the marketing and tactics chapters are light and cover overarching ideas versus in-depth how-tos. However, I have a plethora (I need to start using that word more) of resources and worksheets online that are updated regularly.

Please visit www.oliviaomega.com/beautifullybranded and dig in!

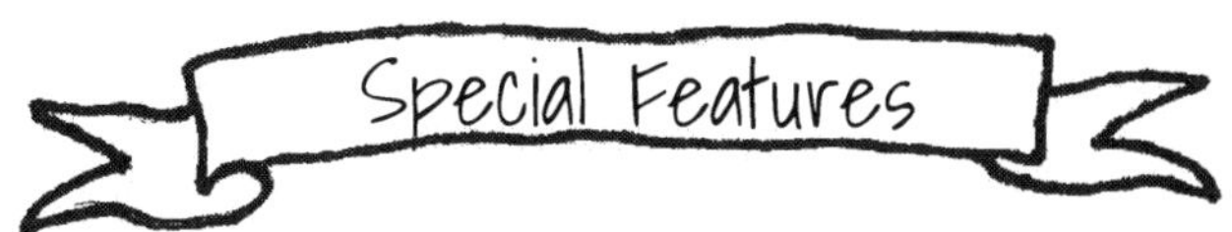

Throughout this book you will find some special elements created with your creative, multi-faceted, imaginative, awesome self in mind! Enjoy!

Quotes from some super smart people that will help motivate you on your journey to establishing Brand You.

Homework assignments (don't worry, these are the fun kind) that will get you thinking.

Checklists so you can have tangible takeaways and feel awesome because you got stuff done (who else loves the act of checking things off like I do?).

Journaling prompts that will foster creativity, get your brilliant ideas onto paper and help you stay unstuck.

Random doodles because...well because doodles are fun! And they are perfectly ok for girls of all ages. There will be plenty of space to add your personal touches.

Song recommendations brought to you by myself and illustrator/ daughter M.J. to inspire and motivate you to dance to the beat of your own brand!

Tons of free tools, resource lists and worksheets that can be found at oliviaomega.com/beautifullybranded

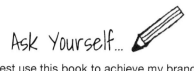

How can I best use this book to achieve my brand and business goals?

Chapter Three

Why for Girls?

Little girls with
dreams become
women with vision.
- unknown

Why for Girls?

I've gotten asked quite a few times why this book is for women and not everyone. This question has only come from men, possibly feeling left out because surely there aren't enough business books written for men by men (wink). My answer is simply...

Why not for girls?

Go to any bookstore and you will find that the selection of business books by women and for women are few. And most shelves are filled with yellow spins insinuating that I'm a dummy. In all honesty, all of the strategies and tactics in this book can be successfully applied by both men and women. My delivery is just unique for my audience. Yes, the topic of personal branding is for everyone, but there is a certain way about a woman. A certain thing we have that men don't. Neither good nor bad, just different. Our anatomy is different. And our ways of thinking, expressing and serving are different.

According to statistics, women are starting businesses at two times the rate of men. Among women, the group launching at the fastest rate are African-American women.

And...

- More than 9.4 million firms are owned by women, employing nearly 7.9 million people, and generating $1.5 trillion in sales as of 2015.

- Women-owned firms (51% or more) account for 31% of all privately held firms and contribute 14% of employment and 12% of revenues.

- 2.9 million firms are majority-owned by women of color in the U.S.

- These firms employ 1.4 million people and generate $226 billion in revenues annually.

- One in five firms with revenue of $1 million or more is woman-owned.

- 4.2% of all women-owned firms have revenues of 1 million or more.

Source: Womenable report commissioned by American Express "OPEN State of Women-Owned Businesses 2015 and NWBC 2015 Annual Report.

While there are plenty of other statistics that show a major lack of women in leadership, education and technology, these numbers let me know that we are making critical strides to make a mark in the marketplace and that we hold a very important role in our economy regardless of our profession or vocation.

Embrace Your Inner Girl

As a woman and mom, it's important for me to embrace my inner girl and not tuck her away simply because she may not be as well liked by society, or she may make others uncomfortable because she's too sensitive, too emotional, too feely, too soft, too connected. These are all things that make us as women so special. We were created this way. Some more so than others of course. But this is the essence of why we are on this earth – to infuse love, life, creativity, interconnectivity and brilliance into corporations, institutions, non-profits, families, relationships and individuals.

Several years ago, my then 9-year-old son summed this concept up perfectly. Unprompted during dinner he said, "I think there should be a woman president. Women just make everything a little nicer." I was floored! How's that for foreshadowing? He's totally right! This isn't an argument of who's better, though it quickly turned into one as my then 12-year-old daughter chimed in and the two went into the standard sibling rivalry session. It's simply about understanding, accepting and leveraging the differences.

Throughout this book, I will be encouraging you to embrace your inner girl by allowing yourself to feel, trusting your intuition and balancing your head and heart. Truly being in touch with who you are, what you offer and what you feel will make you a better entrepreneur, consultant, executive, author, artist, spouse, mom, daughter, sister and friend.

Activist and feminist Eve Ensler, who wrote the play "The Vagina Monologues", gave an amazing TEDx Talk on embracing your inner girl, something our society has taught us to suppress. As women we are conditioned not to be too demanding, bossy, harsh or emotional. Yet this is what makes us unique…our super power. And the capacity for young girls all over the world to be relentless, overcoming adversity and thriving in spite of it, is tremendous.

Being in touch with who you are, what you offer and how you feel make you a better entrepreneur, consultant, executive, author and creator.

#beautifullybranded #innergirl #feelit
@oliviaomega

Save the Drama for Your Mama

Or maybe in this case, it really should be save your mama with your drama! My daughter is filled with it. She is dramatic from the tip of her blinged out crown, down to the tippy toes of her dancing feet. If you looked up the word drama in the dictionary, you would find a picture of my little (now taller than me and wearing my clothes) teenage girl beaming with the brightest brace-filled smile and funky polkadot glasses. Before acquiring a more sophisticated sense of style that I assume most girls adopt their first year of high school, she use to confidently rocks mixed matched socks, her pants were just a tad too short and her outfits rarely match. Still she always walked out the door with a "Watch out world!" attitude and stride.

She always carries around a book (or three) and laughs out loud to her own jokes, especially the ones in her head. She is quirky and silly and sweet and genuine. Loud and joyful... until her world has fallen apart and her "life is crying" (a phrase she started using around age 5). In sixth grade at her middle school track banquet she won the award of "Most likely to push through the pain" which is hilarious because she became known for the most dramatic finishes – tears as she crossed the finish line, stumbling before collapsing on to the ground in pain...and then triumph as her fan club of classmates cheered her on chanting "You can do it!" and "We love you!" Couldn't we all use a fan club of girls screaming and chanting our names every now and again?

Beyond typical dramatics, my daughter is one of the most expressive girls I know. While the term "dramatic" often has a negative connotation, "expressive" is more well-received and may describe the amazing way about her even more.

This is her personal brand! 

And the best thing about her personal brand is that she exudes it to the fullest. Authentically. Unapologetically. Like you and I should.

Now a dignified freshman and an author herself, she is finding coolness in reading, writing and geeking out on all things Harry Potter. And when I need a swift kick in the pants, she is right there to so eloquently and dramatically recite the speeches I've given to her, right back to me. She tells me about how God made me special and how I am courageous and the world needs what I have. The absolute best was when she turned to me and reassured me by saying "Mom, when you are authentically yourself you have no competition!"

A girl after my own heart! 

"I am an example of what is possible when girls from the very beginning of their lives are loved and nurtured by people around them. I was surrounded by extraordinary women in my life who taught me about quiet strength and dignity."
- Michelle Obama

As a 12-year-old, I was skinny, awkward and completely in love with Michael Jackson despite the plastic surgeries that started around that time. It was 1991. Mark Wahlberg was Marky Mark and the number one song was "I Wanna Sex You Up" by Color Me Badd. Beauty and the Beast (the original animation) and Hook were the best movies ever. I had dreams of becoming a fashion designer, spending much of my time making clothes for my dolls, drawing sketches and mailing them into Mattel through their Barbie Fan Club (I'm still waiting to hear back from them). I knew how to sew by then and started my first business at 13 selling decorative stuffed animals in craft stores. They each had little birth certificates and rocked the handmade outfits I designed and made for them. Little did I know, as I was finishing high school, a woman by the name of Maxine Clark would launch the company Build-A-Bear Workshop (which went up for sale last year to the tune of $200 million) and blow my similar enterprise out of the water. No hard feelings Maxine. Love you girl!

What I remember most about that age was that I had my first real desire to be like other girls and to be liked by them. I wanted to fit in. The person who says they absolutely don't care about being accepted or having a place where they feel they belong is most likely lying. This desire is built within our human nature. And this desire is far from bad. Often times the thought of fitting in is strongly criticized in the world of marketing, business and even personal development. In reality, we need to shift our thinking around it. There is nothing wrong with the idea of belonging. This is why we as human beings need and gravitate towards the structure, support and identity of family and community. The focus needs to be on maintaining our individuality and not changing our true innate selves in order to belong. Find belonging in those that embrace you for who you are.

This book is written on the foundation of authenticity as a differentiating benefit and competitive advantage. Our best bet in branding ourselves is to simply be who we are, quirks and all, and to not conform or apologize for it. Needless to say, my daughter is much farther along than I was, having an amazing grasp on this concept. This is something I didn't truly adopt until fairly recently in life. She reminds me everyday that it's okay to be you. And on those days when she forgets, I remind her that she is unique and that God created her exactly the way she is for a very special purpose.

And that special thing that only she has, the world needs from her and her alone.

What quirks and passions did I have as a girl? How can they help me in my business? How can I embrace my inner girl?

Chapter Four

Personal Branding Defined

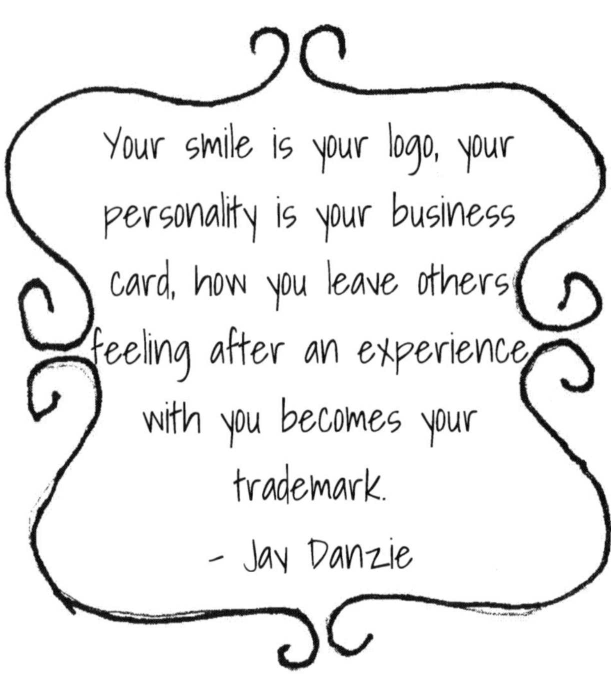
Your smile is your logo, your
personality is your business
card, how you leave others
feeling after an experience
with you becomes your
trademark.
- Jay Danzie

What is Personal Branding?

Let's start at the very beginning, a very good place to start! If you caught my subtle Sound of Music reference then you and I just may be soul sisters!

Instead of starting at the beginning, we often skip straight to color pallets, logo design and website development before we've gotten clear on who we are, what we are offering and the problem we are solving for whom. True brand strategy (not brand identity) and the thinking that goes behind it is the beginning of establishing yourself as an expert.

The definition of a brand is the set of expectations, memories, stories and relationships, visuals, marks and characteristics that, taken together, account for a consumer's decision to choose one product or service over another. If the consumer (whether it's a business, a buyer or a client) doesn't pay a premium, make a selection or spread the word, then no brand value exists for that consumer. That brand's value is determined by the sum total of how much extra people will pay, or how often they choose, the expectations, memories, stories and relationships of one brand over the alternatives.

Take Starbucks for example. I am in love with this brand and have been for many years. Again, we may be soul sisters if you feel the same way! Those non-believers always seem to ask what's so great about Starbucks? Well for starters, it never changes. The consistency is what I love. I don't have to pretend to be something I'm not and the brand accepts me as I am. Heck, I show up un-showered, still in my pajamas with mix-matched socks and Starbucks never says a word. They still give me what I need, no questions asked. And as usual, the coffee is really good. The brand equity I find in Starbucks comes down to two simple elements: brand experience and consistency. The definition of brand experience is: the opportunity for the consumer to "actively engage" with the brand on a personal level through an consistent intimate experience–as opposed to "passively participate" through traditional above-the-line brand messaging.

At age seven, my daughter quickly picked up on all of the elements that make up the Starbucks brand experience - the atmosphere, the company, the service, the music, the smell and even the cup. Oh the cup! "Sitting here at Starbucks, drinking hot cocoa, the people, the music, and this cup in my hand...it makes me feel like a woman," she proudly proclaimed. I couldn't have made up a better quote if I tried!

I use her example in every marketing/branding class I teach. The power of a brand is found in how it makes people feel, not necessarily in what it does. It's all about the emotional needs and wants. After all, my daughter wanted to feel like a woman. :)

People will experience your personal brand through a variety of offline (face-to-face, in-person interactions) and online touch points. Your online touch points include, but are not limited to, website visits, emails, autoresponders, Facebook posts, tweets, photos on Instagram, replies to comments on social media, YouTube videos, profile pictures, your LinkedIn profile and more. Your current a prospective customers will often times "meet you" and experience your brand through these online interactions well before they meet in person (if they have the opportunity to physically meet you at all), making your online brand presence critical and the consistency of that presence crucial.

I love speaking and teaching at conferences for a plethora (there's that word again) of reasons. One of them is the fact that I have an opportunity to interact with and build relationships with large numbers attendees through online touch points before I ever set foot in the city. Through my website, videos and social media posts that speak directly to the conference attendees (hashtags are great for this), my name and face become familiar. They have an experience with me and feel like they know me before we've met. Which is perfect because I've already built preeminence and trust before they hear me speak. It's kind of crazy to go to an event with 500 women you've never "met" before and have people recognize you. That's the power of personal branding!

Now let's take the concept of a brand and apply it to a person. Personal branding is traditionally defined as the process where people and their careers are marked as brands. The personal branding concept suggests that success comes from self-*packaging* (or self-marketing).

The process is further defined as the creation (and then communication) of an asset that pertains to a particular person or individual; this includes but is not limited to their intellectual properties (thinking, theories, teachings, etc.), skills, areas of knowledge or expertise, and even physical appearance (the overall embodiment) leading to a uniquely distinguishable, and ideally memorable, impression. Supposedly the term and concept of personal branding was first used and discussed in an article by Tom Peters called "The Brand Called You". Surprisingly, the points made are still super relevant even after several decades. It's only dated by the brand examples used.

> *It's time for me—and you—to take a lesson from the big brands, a lesson that's true for anyone who's interested in what it takes to stand out and prosper in the new world of work.*
>
> *Regardless of age, regardless of position, regardless of the business we happen to be in, all of us need to understand the importance of branding. We are CEOs of our own companies:*

Me Inc. To be in business today, our most important job is to be head marketer for the brand called You.

A more modern definition of personal branding is how individuals and entrepreneurs differentiate themselves and stand out from a crowd by identifying and articulating their unique value proposition, whether professional or personal, and then leveraging it across platforms with a consistent message and image to achieve a specific goal. In this way, individuals can enhance their recognition as experts in their field, establish reputation and credibility, advance their careers, and build self-confidence. We'll talk more about differentiating benefits and value propositions later in chapter seven, the strategy chapter. Also look for worksheets and videos that will help make these concepts clearer.

If you haven't caught onto the clues yet, let me let you in on a little secret...you are your brand! Yes you! Your name, your face, your personality and your beautiful, amazing story. And don't let anyone (including yourself) convince you otherwise! Often times, we will hide ourselves behind the face of our business or company not realizing that that face should be our own. People do business with people. People fall in love with people. And people are drawn in by the captivating stories of people, not necessarily products, logos and websites.

Our personal brands are stitched together by the unique threads of a beautiful, messy, glorious story.

#beautifullybranded #innergirl #feelit
@oliviaomega

To reiterate and drive this point home (I just have to make sure this really sinks in), you are your brand. One of the best ways I've heard this summed up is that your smile is your logo and your personality is your business card. Your personal self and your professional self are one. Where the two intersect is where your value proposition lies. Where the dynamic qualities of your expertise and the unique qualities of you as a person come together is where you can connect with your most valuable customers. Your brand becomes real, genuine and unbeatable. I know I keep saying it (and I promise you'll hear it again), but when you are your authentic self, your brand has no competition.

Self portrait time...

Draw what you see in the mirror. Your only competition is the person staring back at you!

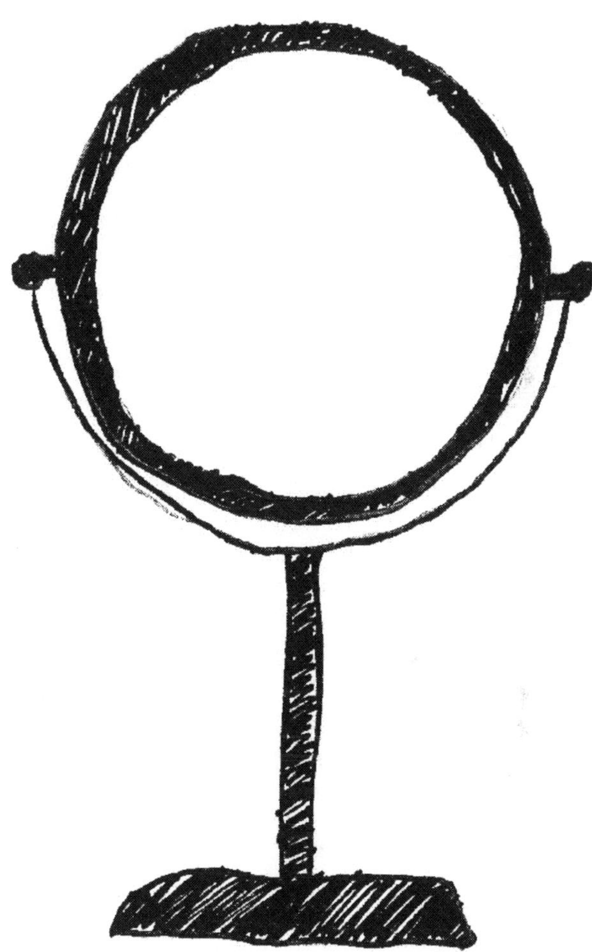

Your to-do list...

- [ ] First and foremost, register the url for your first and last name through a domain provider to use (now or later) to build your brand through a branded website or blog.

  Check out oliviaomega.com/beautifullybranded for a list of resources.

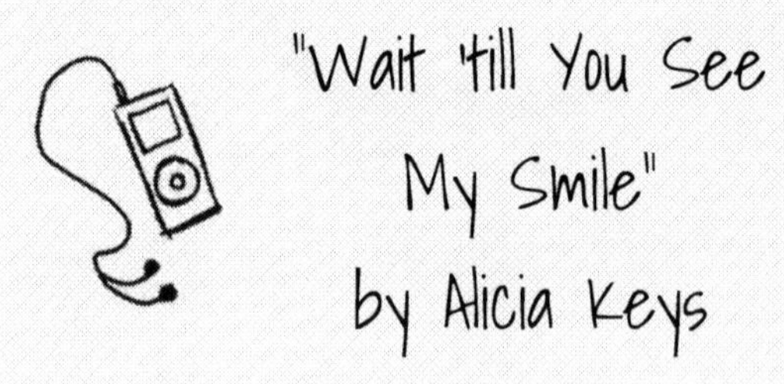

"Wait 'till You See
My Smile"
by Alicia Keys

How have I been trying to separate my personal self from my professional self? How can I start to bring them together?

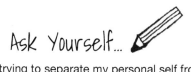

Chapter Five

Your Brand's Anatomy

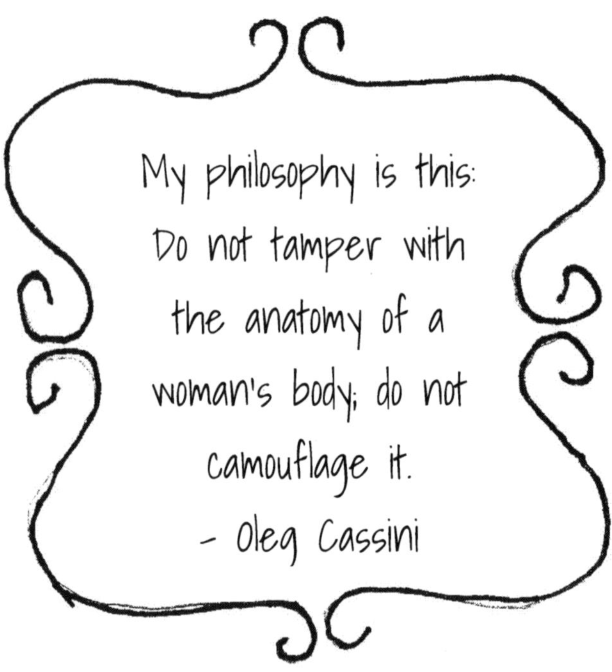
My philosophy is this:
Do not tamper with
the anatomy of a
woman's body; do not
camouflage it.
- Oleg Cassini

A Woman's Anatomy

There was a very specific time in my life when I was at a crossroads in every area – professionally, personally, parentally, passion-ally (what else starts with P and ends in ally?). Everything seemed like it was up in the air, a toss up that could land either way. All I knew was that the decisions I was about to make would lead to possible happiness or despair. My "life was crying" and I needed direction. I called on my Pastor. Know that he is truly like a father to me, having known me over half of my life and seeing me through the biggest ups and downs I've ever faced. So I trust him completely. However, I also know him well enough to know that if I want a coddling shoulder to cry on who will validate my emotions, he is not the one! That's what my girlfriends are for. He focuses on facts and the Word of God alone, NOT feelings.

I met with him to get advice on what to do with my life, personally and professional, fighting the urge to have a dramatic "Malia moment" because that would do no good here. He said exactly what I expected him to say in his super calm, cool and collected voice…"Everything will be fine, daughter." And "You'll know what to do. Just trust God." That voice is so reassuring and yet is so frustrating because there is nothing calm about your life crying.

Then he said something completely unexpected. Something I will never forget. He said, "Release the barracuda." Wait, what?! All I could think about was the scene in Charlie's Angels where Lucy Lui marches in like a boss to the song "Barracuda" by Heart, wearing head-to-toe black leather. No, this scene had nothing to do with his advice. Though later I did add a black leather skirt, pants and bustier to my wardrobe. Nothing snaps you out of feeling like a tired, worn out mom like leather!

What he was referring to were the characteristics of the barracuda. But for all intensive purposes, he was telling me to BE FIERCE in the only way that I know how.

The barracuda is fierce in both looks and behavior, and it uses aggressive strategies to overtake its prey. They are not shy and don't play around when it comes to getting what they want and need. Barracudas are selfish, ferocious and opportunistic. They are competitive in nature and defeat both prey and enemies by simply biting them in half. Dang! More importantly, the barracuda strategically uses every element of their anatomy, instincts and DNA to get what they are after. The synergies created by simultaneously using everything in their God-given nature (who they were created to be) allow them to conquer and dominate.

So it's time ladies!
Release your secret weapon! It's in your DNA...

Your personal brand becomes profitable when you can utilize what's inside your DNA to uniquely showcase your expertise and connect to your target audience.

#beautifullybranded #personalbranding
@oliviaomega

So that's what I did! I released it. All of it!

I quit my job. I quit my boyfriend. I kept my kids. And I started on a journey to do and be what I was meant to. I was going to start asking for what I wanted out of life and demanding what I needed. By combining and utilizing everything in my DNA, I would start to dominate in all of the desires of my heart. In that moment, I realized that this is what personal branding allows us to do. And when broken down, personal branding resembles our body's anatomy.

Your personal brand is made up of several self-contained, however not self-sufficient parts. These elements make up the most critical pieces of your brand.

They include the heart, head, gut (these three combined create the brand's core), arms and hands, legs and feet, and how we dress (literally and figuratively).

Each one of these pieces of your anatomy must work together to successfully build a personal brand that showcases your expertise, sets you apart from others in your field and brings you profitable clients and contracts.

Your Personal Brand Anatomy

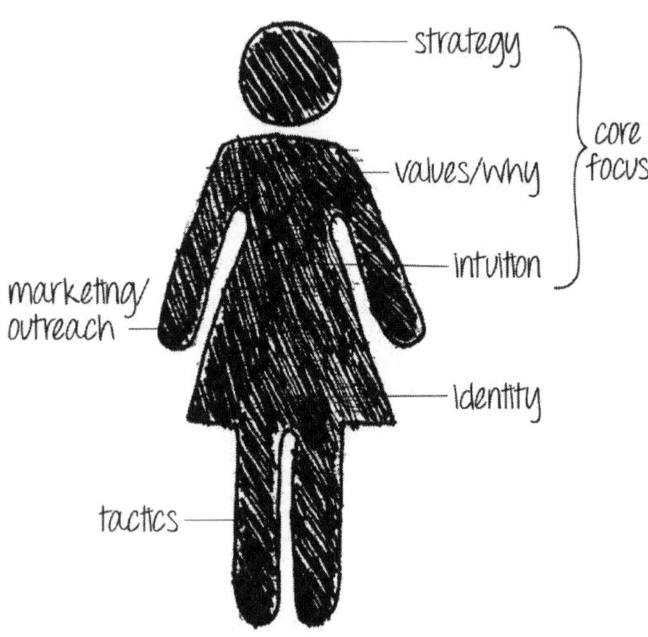

Your Heart – Values/Why

The heart represents who you are and what your brand stands for. It encompasses your passions, emotions, feelings which make up your truest authentic self.

Your Head - Strategy

The head or the brain of your personal brand is the strategy. The head tells all of the other body parts what to do and where to go - with purpose. There is a vision, goals and thought process behind everything that the body does in service of the brand.

Your Gut - Intuition

Otherwise known as your instincts, this area of your brand is critical when deciphering the often conflicting opinions of the head and heart, requiring a "gut check". When in doubt, trust your gut...it's always right!

Your Core – Focus

Combined, the heart, head and gut make up the most important and synergistic element of your brand. At the core of who you are lies the answers to who you should serve (your target audience) and exactly what you should offer them (your niche and expertise). Your core directs your brand's voice and message. It's what's at your core that makes you authentic and unique.

Your Hands – Marketing/Outreach

They represent the marketing of your personal brand and the building of relationships including social media and outreach strategies. It also encompasses the strategic partnerships and collaborations you'll need to create in order to be successful.

Your Feet - Tactics

The legs and feet of your personal brand represent the actual tactics and programs that once executed, will get you from point A to point B. This is all about execution. Walk it out!

Your Dress (cape) - Identity

This is your brand's visual identity and packaging. It includes your logo, business cards, and online graphics, all the way down to how you dress. Being comfortable in your skin will be key in presenting an authentic brand.

"Let excellence be your brand... When you are excellent, you become unforgettable."
- Oprah Winfrey

The rest of this book will address each element of your personal brand anatomy in more depth so you can get a better understanding of the purpose of each body part. Implementation of the knowledge and strategies shared will ensure success in building a personal brand that resonates with your perfect target market, positions you as THE expert in you field, eliminates competition (there's only one you) and drives revenue for your business.

To help frame your brand, begin to think about "THE ONE THING" that you would want to me known for across the world. What one thing will people automatically and consistently associate with you? What is at the heart of your DNA?

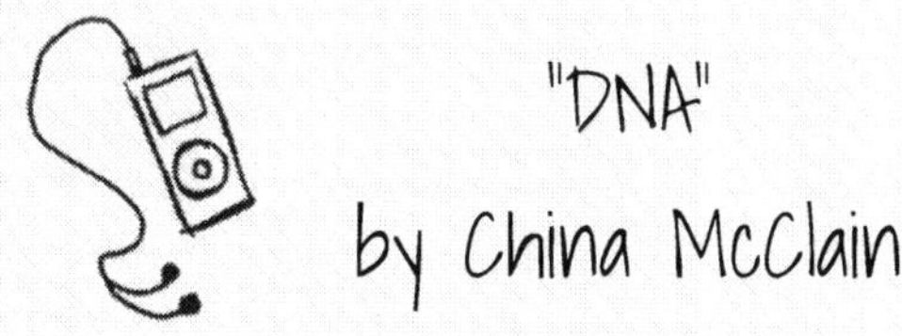

Are there parts of my DNA (at the core of who I am) that I can leverage in my personal brand?

Chapter Six

Your Heart

Establish A Pulse & Purpose

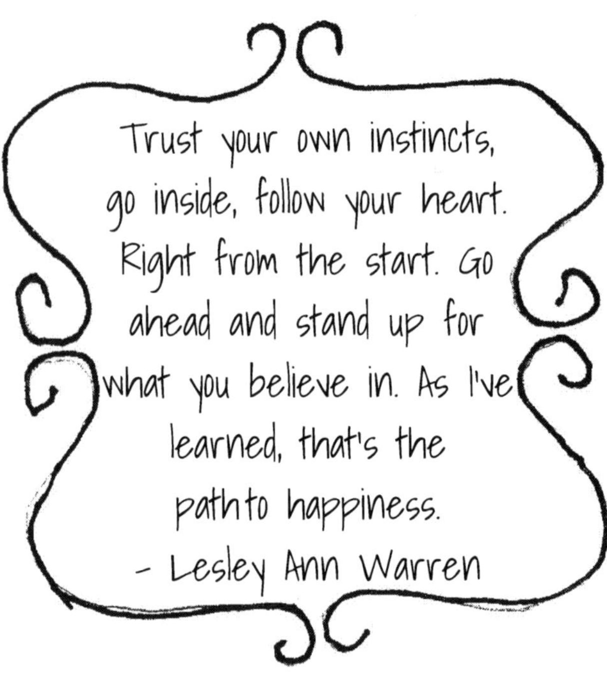
Trust your own instincts,
go inside, follow your heart.
Right from the start. Go
ahead and stand up for
what you believe in. As I've
learned, that's the
pathto happiness.
- Lesley Ann Warren

Your Heart

Oh, the heart! If you've ever been in love, you know the power that it holds; the power to turn lives upside down for the better and sometimes for the worse. It is both powerful and vulnerable at the same time. Here resides the passion that drives you to do what you do and to serve who you serve. Your WHY.

Why you do what you do should be determined and articulated before you formulate your what (strategy), how (tactics), who (target) and so on.

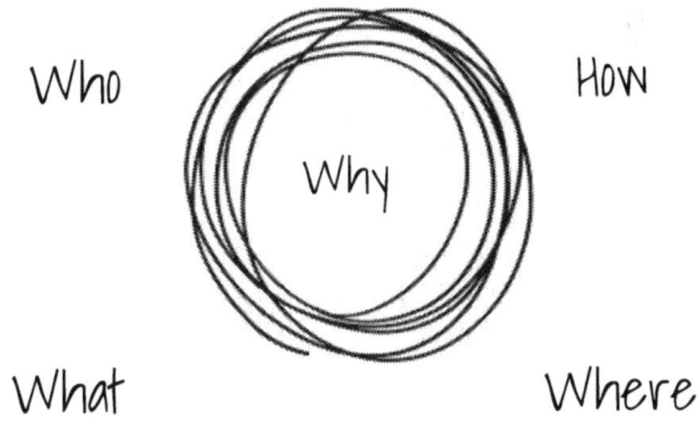

Your answer to the question "Why?" reveals what lives in your heart and what your values are. That answer needs to be emotive (attached to a deep emotional need) versus functional (attached to a tangible need). You can get to this answer by asking yourself why you want to do what you want to do (become an author, start a school, start a business, found a non-profit). Once you answer that first question, ask “why” again. And again. This is so much harder than you would think. If it were easy, we would all be clear on our purpose and never be distracted or discouraged. Continue to ask yourself “why” until you can no longer answer the question.

The goal is to ladder up or elevate to an answer that reveals what you feel your purpose on this earth is. Deep isn’t it? It has to be deep to motivate you to push hard, grind and never give up even when it seems impossible. Your “why” is stable and grounded, it isn’t fleeting and doesn’t change day to day like our feelings can. Your heart beats for this reason.

The way you express your "why" and the way you serve your target is your personal brand's love language. In the book popular book "The Five Love Languages" by Gary Chapman, the idea that we each have our own language used to show our love and affection to another reveals the uniqueness of our individual brands. No one can show love quite like you do. This is your gift. This is your competitive edge.

According to Chapman, the five love languages include words of affirmation, quality time, receiving gifts, acts of service and physical touch. While these aren't always directly applicable, they apply indirectly to every way in which you serve your clients as well as to each touch point in which they experience your brand.

If you've ever heard me speak, you'll know that I'm notorious for using dating analogies to bring to life concepts around marketing and branding. Possibly because my first real dating experiences took place as a single mom in my mid-thirties. So here goes! In love, you're always going to lose if you make decisions solely from your head, based only on logic. The same goes with your heart. Acting simply based on how you feel can be detrimental. In a perfect world and in any perfect relationship (those exist right?), you will have a balance of love and logic. Your personal brand should live in this magical world of blissful balance. The head (strategy) and the heart (values) engage in a beautiful two-step, dancing in such a way where they take turns leading and following, never straying far from the other.

Your values are who you are at the center of your being. This doesn't change. While the ebbs and flows of life may shift our focus from time to time and our business offerings may change, our value stay pretty consistent. Determine what your values are and exude them to death! They should ooze out of your pores, out of everything you write, create, produce and publish. No one should ever have to wonder or question what you stand for. When we get into the habit of hiding this part of ourselves from our clients, fans and followers, we present a bland, vanilla version of ourselves...possibly liked by many, but never really loved by any.

If you like ice cream as much as I do, you'll find that vanilla is a core flavor. It's the base flavor for many flavors. But when asked what your absolute favorite ice cream flavor is, people rarely say vanilla. This example went south when someone in my workshop genuinely preferred vanilla over any other flavor. But you get the point. You want to be the super thick and chunky rocky road that people either LOVE or don't care for at all. Trying to please everyone, not offend and appeal to the majority of people makes you a vanilla (plain) brand.

When you are consistently your true self, no one has to question if you're genuine. Examine your personality and what you are known for within your circle of friends, family and colleagues. If you're serious by nature, then be serious. If you're silly or sarcastic, embrace that and use it to your advantage. If you value your relationship with God, then let your light shine for the world to see. Don't hide it! If you have a weird obsession with shoes, play it up to it's fullest and use your obsession to connect with your audience. If they can't relate to your shoe fetish or are turned off by your three massive shoe closets, then they probably aren't your target.

Every few miles on the road of entrepreneurship, take a moment to dig deep and remember who you are, what you stand for and who you serve. This is your personal brand.

#beautifullybranded #personalbranding
@oliviaomega

We've all done it…seeing how we stack up next to our competition, sizing up someone else's blog, comparing ourselves to an ex's new girlfriend (or new wife for that matter), placing ourselves in a side-by-side face off of who's the best. In this type of battle, I will always lose for several reasons. First, the competition really only exists in my head so I'm both the judge and the jury. You'll never win when the one who makes the call is your worst critic – yourself.

A second common mistake I make is comparing myself to others based on criteria that I can't control. Let's take boobs for example. We're talking about anatomy right? You've either got 'em or you don't. Blessed or not so much. I'm in the latter camp. And there isn't a whole lot you can really do about it. You could go the expensive route and get implants or you can throw on a push up bra and call it a day. Focusing on things that are out of our control is a pointless waste of energy and it starts to negatively impact our mood, confidence and even our results.

Entrepreneurs in your similar field should serve as a source of motivation and inspiration, fueling you to keep growing and to be your very best. When other business owners start to create in you self-doubt, insecurities and a lack of motivation, it's time to examine yourself closely and remember that you were created uniquely special, unlike anyone else.

You were made for a very special purpose, with a calling and vision that is all your own. As discussed in the last chapter, we each have a physical DNA that can't be duplicated. But we also have an entrepreneurial DNA. It flows through our bloodstream and the same exact makeup doesn't exist within anyone else. When you begin to fully grasp the power within your uniqueness and the priceless value of your gifts and talents, you can compete on a level where no one can touch you. You have no competition because there is no other you in this world. Discovering your true self, staying true to that true self and then expressing it to the world (through personal branding) will give you an unstoppable edge, strategically positioning you in a place where you have no competition.

Attract or repel. If they don't love you, they are not your target.

#lawofattraction #personalbranding
@oliviaomega

After reading this book remember that your brand should both attract and repel people. Not play it too safe. If you stay true to your heart and wear it on your sleeve for the world to see, they will either love you or hate you for it. It definitely takes courage to become vulnerable in a public space, letting your fan base, blog readers, class attendees and peers into the depths of who you are as a person. But face it, no one falls in love with blah people or brands for that matter. A watered down, lukewarm brand won't catch the attention of potential customers and it won't keep the loyalty of current ones. Exposing what lies in your heart (even some things that may be buried a bit deep in there) is what will build solid relationships. Your heart is the key!

Awww...now we're getting all mushy and gushy! I'm sure some of you feel right at home. But if all this lovey dovey talk makes you uncomfortable, the next chapter will make you feel much better.

> "My writing, like everything I do, comes profoundly from my heart. I believe that if you follow your heart you will be successful in one way or another."
> – Kim Elizabeth

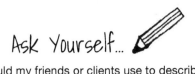

What 3 words would my friends or clients use to describe me?
What values do I possess that can shape my vision/mission?

Your to-do list...

☐ Create your own personal manifesto which is a written statement declaring your life's purpose, values and intentions regarding how you live day-to-day, what you stand for.

This should be created using your brand positioning statement from chapter five as the foundation.

☐ Make a vision board that incorporates elements from your manifesto, using visuals to set the mood or tone for your brand.

Pinterest is a great resource for both tasks.

Chapter Seven

Your Head

The Bling & Brains of Your Brand

Follow your heart
but bring your
head with you.
- Alfred Adler

Your Head

The head or the brain of your personal brand and business is your strategy. Hey analytical thinks, you'll start to feel a bit more comfortable now. Your heart is key, but I can't stress enough that strategy is key...too. Whether building a personal brand or branding a small business, it always has to start with vision and therefore strategy - the main means you'll use to get from point A to point B. Contrary to popular belief, this is the most important element of branding (not your logo) and yet it is the main thing that gets overlooked. The strategy is what guides the ship, it includes the compass that helps navigate the path and get you to where you want to go. It involves visioning, goal setting and defining a brand's purpose.

Your brand strategy details how you intend to offer value, create customers and stand out beyond the reach of your competitors through differentiating benefits. The strategy leads to smart, intentional planning that sets forth the creative, social and moral steps the brand will take drive the business forward.

I was fortunate enough to be "raised" in an advertising and brand-positioning agency where everything started with strategy. Even a simple logo design began with an in-depth look at the brand's strategic direction, market landscape, industry conditions and competitive set. It wasn't just any strategy, but informed strategy that began with research and consumer insights.

Nothing is more important than to have a clear direction of where you're going and why. Without a blueprint, it is impossible to build a house. And without strategy, tactics are purposeless. As cliché as it may sound, it's definitely true that without vision the people will perish.

This is exactly what happens to many of our dreams. We set out on the great adventure of making our dream of becoming a great speaker, artist, author, coach, counselor and entrepreneur come true. We're filled with more enthusiasm, optimism, courage and energy than we could have imagined. In our enthusiasm, we quickly set out to pick a logo, order business cards and build a DIY website without stopping to think about the ultimate vision for our business, our brand, ourselves.

And we've all become tongue tied, when our friends ask us what we do. We fumble on our words because there are so many amazing things swirling around in our brilliantly scattered, attention-challenged, entrepreneurial minds. It's not that we don't know who we are or what we do, it's simply because we haven't taken the time to sit down and map it out.

This is where vision is critical. How can you get from point A to point B if you don't know where point B is? Your brand's strategy is made up of your vision, purpose and goals.

Before you can dive into mapping out a strategy, let's do some digging and soul searching to determine who you are in your market and what your strengths and weaknesses consist of. If you went to business school or ever took a marketing class, then you know what a S.W.O.T. analysis is. Traditionally, it is a structured planning method and strategic process used to evaluate the Strengths, Weaknesses, Opportunities, and Threats involved in a project or business.

The purpose of a personal S.W.O.T. is to analyze your personal brand – yourself as a service provider, strategic solution and problem solver for your clients.

Personal Brand S.W.O.T. Analysis

Personal and professional STRENGTHS (internal)	Personal and professional WEAKNESSES (internal)
OPPORTUNITIES within your industry that you can leverage (external)	THREATS within your industry that may hinder you (external)

This tool will help you more clearly understand how you stack up against your competitive set and alternatives – the other viable options that can be chosen over what you personally provide.

The notion of doing a personal S.W.O.T. can be tricky for some especially since it's more commonly done for a company. It can be extremely hard for us to step outside of our bodies and take an objective external look at ourselves, truly evaluating our personal assets and liabilities. It's even more difficult, yet more beneficial to do it in a way that combines our personal selves seamlessly with our professional selves.

There are some tricks to completing a S.W.O.T. So here are some tips to help you complete this critical step:

Combine your personal and professional selves

When evaluating your strengths and weaknesses, don't just look at what you do on a professional level. Also, look at where you thrive and where you may fall short on a personal level as well. Where these two areas intersect or overlap is where your most unique qualities reside.

You are your brand. So your abilities in your personal life and your personality traits play a large role in how you treat your customers and the unique value proposition that you provide them. If you are a mom, for example, patience may be one of your strengths and therefore a differentiating benefit that will prove to be an asset to your clients. Being a woman in itself is part of your brand and is a huge competitive edge!

Recruit some help

Enlist a combination of your friends, colleagues, business partners and current or past clients to help you capture your strengths and weaknesses. Ask them to write a quick sentence or two about how you have added value to their lives, business or project and what makes you unique. Ask them what you do or provide that no one else can do. And ask them how you make them feel (getting at the emotional benefits you provide, not just the functional ones). What stresses do you help them relieve? By getting a combination of personal and professional testimonials, you can tap into your truest self expression and that sweet spot where your personal self and professional self overlap.

Examine each weakness

We can all be extremely critical of ourselves so it shouldn't surprise you when it's easier to come up with a list of weaknesses compared to strengths. But what we have to realize is that sometimes our most unique value proposition fall within what appears to be a weakness, flipped to our advantage. Speaker and researcher Brené Brown (who I love by the way) talks about this in her book *The Gifts of Imperfection: Letting Go of Who You Think You're Supposed to Be and Embracing Who You Are*. For my personal S.W.O.T., I listed "lack of focus" as one of my weaknesses. As a creative entrepreneur, I'm constantly finding my mind wandering, dreaming up my next big project, business launch or book, making it difficult at times to focus on the tasks at hand. Can I get an amen?! I know you've been there. While this is a weakness in many cases, it's also one of my strengths – being creative, never complacent, dreaming big (for myself and my clients) and seeing the potential for new ventures is a special gift that not everyone possesses.

"Imperfection is beauty, madness is genius and it's better to be absolutely ridiculous than absolutely boring."

- Marilyn Monroe

Your Personal Brand S.W.O.T. Analysis

"Be confident. Too many days are wasted comparing ourselves to others and wishing to be something we aren't. Everybody has their own strengths and weaknesses, and it is only when you accept everything you are, and aren't, that you truly succeed." - unknown

"Flawless"
by Beyoncé
clean version :)

Where do you want to be in 5 years? What goals will get you there? What weaknesses can you turn into strengths?

Your to-do list...

- [ ] Complete your personal brand S.W.O.T. analysis
- [ ] Fill out your annual Goals, Intentions and Declarations tool kit to get clear on your vision for your brand and business
- [ ] Literally map out your SMART goals (Specific, Measurable, Attainable, Relevant, Time-based) for the year, quarter and month

These worksheets and more can be found at www.oliviaomega.com/beautifullybranded

Chapter Eight

Your Gut

A Woman's Intuition

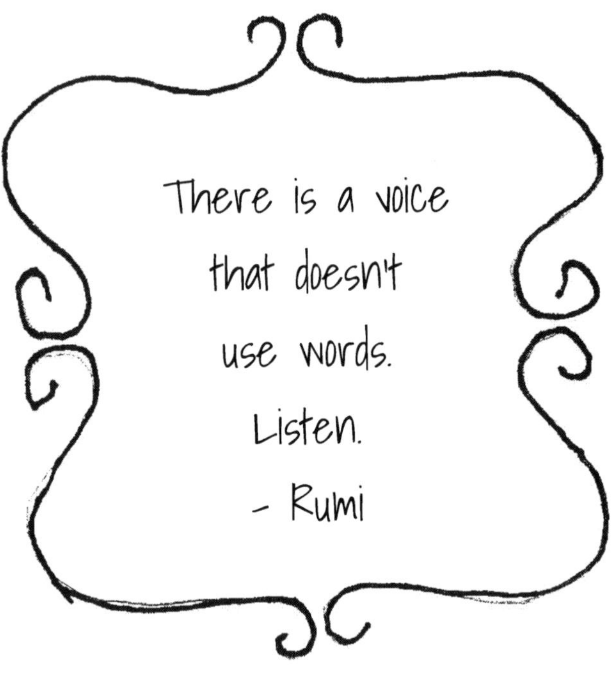
There is a voice
that doesn't
use words.
Listen.
- Rumi

Your Gut

Something told me to write to The Ellen Show. It was a crazy idea and had about a 5% chance of working, but I couldn't shake the feeling. It was two weeks after I left my corporate job to take care of my one-year-old son who had been sick. I figured while I was home with him and not working I could turn the baby gifts I was making for friends into a business. I didn't have a supplier, formal manufacturing process or website yet, but I had a name and an idea...for Ellen. Without thinking it all the way through, I quickly created a sample of customized baby onesies (later I would learn through a cease and desist letter that this word is trademarked by Gerber), wrote out my story, attached a picture of me and my kids, and proceeded to the post office with said kids.

I knew that my product's cute concept and original packaging had stopping power, but it wasn't going to stop anything in a sea of fan mail. That's right, I send my Mother's Day show pitch to the fan mail address I found on the website. It's all I had. And it was a long shot. This is where my head kicked in...right in the middle of the line at the post office. "Who am I to pitch Ellen DeGeneres? I don't even have an actual business yet. And I don't even have a name or a real address to send this to. I'm sure they get thousands of pieces of fan mail a week." The negative thinking and doubt were pouring into my head just as fast as my heart was beating.

If that wasn't enough, my arm began to cramp from holding the baby in a line that didn't seem to move and I lost sight of my toddler who I found her laying on the floor of the post office singing a Dora The Explorer song (I've never been so happy for my kids to transition out of a stage). Who was I fooling? I promise you, I was so close to turning around and going home. My brain had all of the reasons why it would never work. And it was past nap time. But my heart kept saying "but what if.."

I figured the worse that could happen was that my shirts end up in the abyss of Ellen fan mail without a single reply and I would waste thirty dollars on product and shipping. In that moment, my head and heart were playing tug of war and I needed a tie breaker.

It was my gut – that feeling in the pit of my stomach that in reality was a combination of nausea, hunger and sleep deprivation. But it felt right! I'm sure you've experienced this as an entrepreneur. A feeling you can't quite explain. As women, we all have it…it's our intuition. My candy-wrapped baby shirts ended up being featured on The Ellen Show not one, not two, but three years in a row! I would say my little hunch was well worth the wait in line.

This section of the book is pretty self-explanatory so we won't spend too much time here, but it must be addressed. A woman's intuition is strong, undeniable and it's very rarely wrong. This is where the head and the heart meet. A beautiful balancing act of love and logic.

It's in this part of the anatomy, the gut, that we can feel an unexplainable peace about something or an unsettling restlessness that is difficult to put into words. As much as we would like to rely solely on either clear thought processes or what makes our hearts skip a beat, there is a third element that can act as the tie breaker when the head and heart don't see eye to eye.

I've often wondered where our instinct comes from. For me, it's that gentle yet clear whisper from God that directs or steers me down a certain path. It can literally be a feeling in my stomach that says "This is not for you" or "You are safe here." Society has taught women to ignore their instincts and to rely on logic. How many times have you been told by co-workers, family and friends to think it through or give it some more thought? This is especially true when we are about to do something that may seem rushed, risky or downright crazy. Sounds like the life of an entrepreneur doesn't it!

What we must remember is that our instinct is rooted in feelings, not thoughts. Which is why justifying actions when they are driven by our intuition is extremely difficult. But in reality, when you follow your gut, no one can tell you you're wrong (or at least they shouldn't). It takes some practice, but with regard to all decisions made for your brand and your business, you must trust your instincts. And, taking it a step further as a woman, you can leverage this innate sense to better serve your target audience.

"There will be a few times in your life when all your instincts will tell you to do something, something that defies logic, upsets your plans, and may seem crazy to others. When that happens, you do it. Listen to your instincts and ignore everything else. Ignore logic, ignore odds, ignore the complications, and just go for it."
- Judith McNaught

What do you feel called to do but that seems crazy to others?
What is your gut saying about the direction you are going in?

Chapter Nine

Your Core

Focus on the Foundation

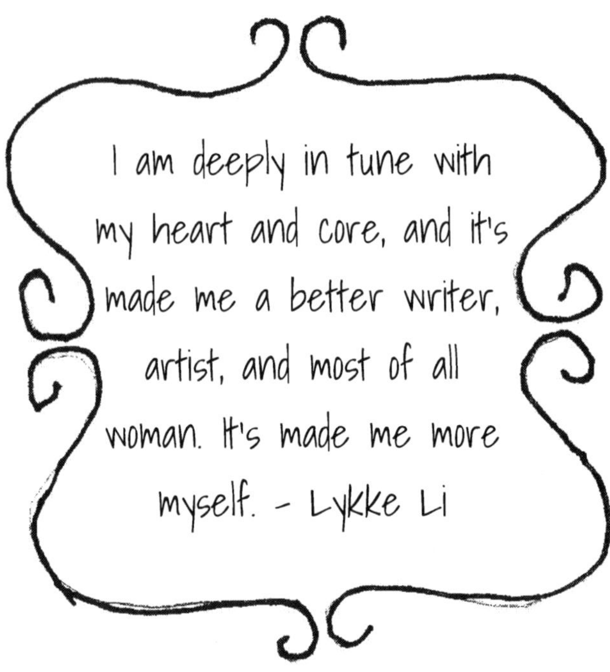
I am deeply in tune with
my heart and core, and it's
made me a better writer,
artist, and most of all
woman. It's made me more
myself. - Lykke Li

Your Core

At the core of your being, you have a skill, an undeniable talent that makes up your unique value. This place is made up of the three most important elements of your brand combined – your heart, head and gut. When they align like the stars, you can truly grasp your purpose. The joy that is experienced when you start walking in that purpose is priceless! This can only be when you narrow in on your niche and focus on solving a very specific problem for a very specific set of people.

I have a picture that I reference all the time of my daughter after her first dance recital around age 6. The expression on her face is that of pure joy! Ridiculous joy!

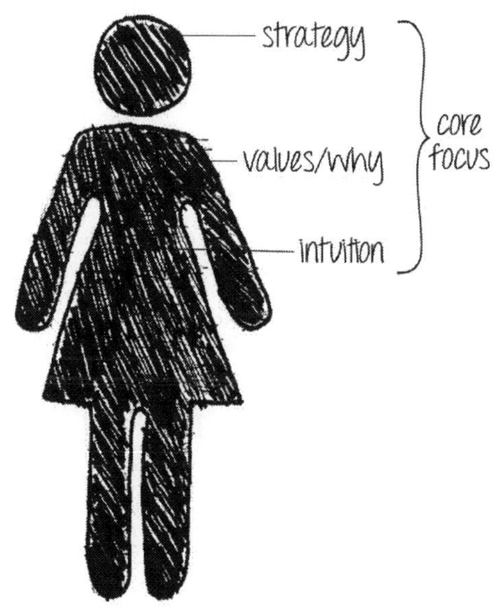

THIS is my reference for what our faces should look like when we do what we absolutely love, which comes from focusing on who we are at our core. Do you remember the last time you were beaming?

I'll never forget this day. It was right after she got off the stage. I'm not sure if was the newness of putting on tons of makeup, the sequins and ruffles of the costume or the energy of the audience, but the pure joy that radiated off of her face was magical. Her cheeks had to have hurt from the intensity of her smile (that lasted for days I might add). From that moment on, her dad and I knew she was destined to be on stage entertaining the masses. This is how we should all look when we go with our gut, follow our dreams and do what we love.

If your face doesn't radiate like this at least some of the time (not all of the time because trust me, I have chronic resting stink face that I have to continuously work on), then you need to change up what you're doing with your life. My face gets pretty darn close to this (or at least I think it looks that way to others...I hope) when I have the opportunity to stand up and speak to women entrepreneurs about personal branding, building a business or the adventures of entrepreneurship. This is what brings me joy...and where I feel at home, in my zone, flowing in my life's purpose. Therefore, this is what I need to do more of!

Ask yourself...what brings you the most joy? And then simply figure out a way to do more of it! I guarantee that what brings you the most joy also brings the most joy and satisfaction to your clients and customers. Win-win!

In order to land on what this is for you, look at several areas in your life, then start to examine where they overlap:

- What you love to do
- What you are good at doing
- What you get paid to do
- What the world needs more of

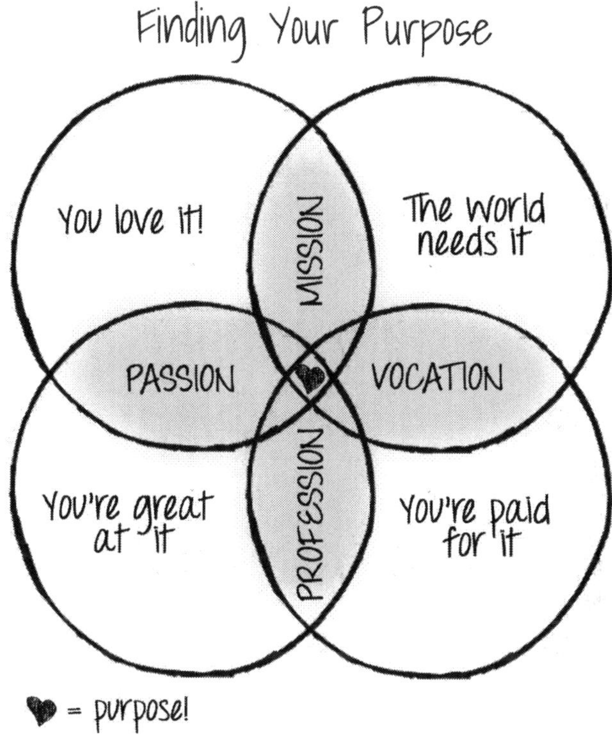

#beautifullybranded #personalbranding #purpose
@oliviaomega

"Never apologize for being sensitive or emotional. Let this be a sign that you've got a big heart and aren't afraid to let others see it. Showing your emotions is a sign of strength."

- Brigitte Nicole

"Wild Things"
by Alessia Cara

What would I do or create even if I never got paid for it? When I feel the most fulfilled in life, what type of work am I doing?

Chapter Ten

Your Hands

Connect Your Brand to Others

Reach out and touch
somebody's hand.
Make this world a
better place
if you can.
- Diana Ross

Your Hands

Once the personal brand has been defined, it's time to communicate that brand to the world, but more specifically, market to the specific target that will be able to receive it. Narrowing down your target audience is critical to your success.

Casting the widest net to the broadest possible audience is a sure way to catch the riff raff of the sea. Instead, decide exactly what you want to catch then use the specific bait that will draw them in.

Think about who your tribe is and exactly who you want to attract. This is more than demographic, but also psychographics. What do they do in their free time? Where do they like to shop? What brands do they wear? Are there brands that they already love and follow that you can partner with? Where do they hang out online? What worries and problems keep them up at night that you can solve?

With the ever evolving world of marketing, I want to make sure I offer you the most updated resources available so please visit the website for more tools to help you narrow down your target and then market to them where they are already hanging out.

"I really believe that when you give people authentic identity, which is what [social media] does, and you can be your real self and connect with real people online, things will change." - Sheryl Sandberg

"I'm Coming Out" by Diana Ross

What social sites does my ideal client use most? Where do they seek info about my industry/product? What are their concerns?

Chapter Eleven

Your Feet

Time to Walk Out Your Plan

Strategy without tactics is
the slowest route to
victory. Tactics without
strategy is the noise
before defeat.
- Sun Tzu

Your Feet

Here we go! It's time to take action. This is done by determining which steps you will take to execute on your strategy and achieve your goals. A foundation of vision, goals and strategy was laid down at the beginning to know exactly where you are wanting to go. Where you're starting from is point A and where you want to go is point B. The way you get there is completely up to you and is the strategy that you will put in place. Your tactics are the steps and actions you will do to execute your plan.

An entire second book could be written on how to write a marketing plan and the many tactics to choose from. More details and up-to-date list of viable tactics and resources are on the website for you to reference and download.

"Don't sit down and wait for the opportunity to come. Get up and make them."

- Madam CJ Walker

"Opportunity"

by Quvenzhane Walls

What social platforms am I currently using, love and can make a priority? What post have my audience responded to most?

Chapter Twelve

Your Dress
The Uniqueness of Your Identity

Style is a way
to say who you
are without
having to speak.
- Rachel Zoe

Your Dress & Identity

A campaign came out several years ago that will forever change the way both men and women see the average bathroom sign…which also happens to be the iconic symbol used throughout this book. The campaign proclaimed "It was never a dress" and shows what we've been looking at the sign all wrong. She isn't wearing a girly dress, she's sporting a super hero cape, representing strength, bravery and superpowers. The cape exemplifies what women are all about! We all have Wonder Woman inside of us somewhere. We are pretty darn super and have the powers, talents, gifts and skills to back it up. These powers go far beyond our looks.

As girls growing up we've heard many times and even teach our daughters that beauty is only skin deep and what really matters is on the inside. This is true and a very important concept to grasp at a young age. When you're building a successful business and brand, what you "look" like is a direct reflection of the type and level of value you bring to the marketplace.

I once had someone tell me that showcasing my face all over my website and business cards could come across as conceited, self-centered and arrogant. They even strongly advised me not to put my face on this book. "Only celebrities do that" they said. Well, I guess I'm going to need to be a celebrity in my own right then.

As discussed toward the beginning of this book, your smile is your logo. While you're beginning to build your brand, you want people to start to remember you. And often times, people may forget a name, but they won't forget your face, which is one of the main elements of your identity. So flaunt it! Everywhere!

If you are building your personal brand, remember that your face is literally the face of your brand. So flaunt it! Everywhere!

#beautifullybranded #personalbranding #identity
@oliviaomega

I hate the phrase "don't judge a book by it's cover"! What!? That's just ridiculous! I always pick up a book based on how well the cover catches my attention. And I always pick wine based on how pretty the label is. Would you feel as great about your purchase of an iPad if it were sold in a run down, cheap, beat up cardboard box? Of course not. Apple is known for their sleek, clean, expensive packaging. It makes you feel special when you open their products.

Packaging is everything. Perception is everything.

The same goes for your personal brand. How you "package" and present yourself represents the contents of that package – your expertise, talents, services, value, etc. Whether you know it or like it, your current and potential clients are judging your value based on your outward appearance (online and in person). Ouch! I know it doesn't feel good, but it's true.

This is human nature. We can't help it.

So examine your entire packaging, not just your wardrobe. How you dress for client meetings, presentations, networking event, even the grocery store (yikes, I really need to take my own advice here). What are you communicating about the contents of your package and the value you offer?

Cheap
Easy (don't make me break out the dating analogies!)
Fast (with regard to speed!)
Laid Back
Immature
Thrown Together
Unorganized
Careless
Carefree
Boring
Out Dated

What would you like current and potential clients to perceive about you based on your packaging?

Poised
Professional
Experienced
Mature
Expensive/Valuable
High Quality
Classy
Daring

Fun
Detail Oriented
Current/Relevant

Here's the challenge... Every morning after you get dressed, stand in the mirror and determine the top three characteristics or adjectives that come to mind when you evaluate what you're wearing. If you feel good about attaching these descriptors to your brand, then you are good to go! If not, reevaluate.

And of all the parts to our physical brand packaging, our nails are one of the easiest things to neglect. Hear me out. Especially as a mom who works from home. When my kids were much younger, finding time fit in a shower was a big deal. If I could get them cleaned, dressed and fed I was doing pretty good.

Think about this scenario – you're pitching a new client over coffee and your nails are a hot mess. Broken or chipped and peeling. Sadly, people make assumptions based on the strangest and smallest of things when they don't know you yet. Which is why first impressions can make or break your business.

I once sat through an entire meeting with my hands under the table because of how embarrassed I was about my nails. I felt like a 12 year old. They literally looked just like my daughter's (we decided to be twins)...hot pink with glitter and majorly chipped to the point where some nails were completely bare. OMG! I wanted so bad to clear the air and blurt out "The condition of my nails is absolutely no indication of the quality of the work I will do for you, my work ethic or attention to detail. I promise." Note that color says a lot as well. My neon pink glitter "Jem Truly Outrageous" (80's babies represent!) nail polish definitely didn't express sophistication. My brand's go-to nail polish color is bright red. If you're the type of gal who never wears polish, try a clear coat. Just not a chipped hot mess.

Let's move onto other elements of our identity. Even with the advancements of technology and the changes in the way we connect, network and socialize, business cards are still the business! This is especially the case when you're in a creative industry where texture, thickness, color and touch are so important. Have you ever been handed a business card...BAM...and you thought to yourself "WHOA, they must be a big deal" simply due to the feel of the card and visual impact? On the flip side, have you ever been handed a business card and you thought to yourself "EW" simply because of the flimsy stock, clipart graphics and poor printing? Business cards, next to your face are more often than not your first impression. Why not knock 'em dead? In addition to making sure they are "beautifully branded" and visually represent who you are, here are some important things to remember when developing your business cards.

Your Face is Your Logo

So show it off! In a room filled with hundreds of faces it's easy to get lost or simply forgotten (our brains simply can't remember it all). While some people shy away from it, I highly recommend putting your beautiful mug on your business card. When people walk away they are much more likely to remember your face when they get home or later that week or that month. It will trigger the amazingly engaging conversation they had with you way better than your name, website url or Twitter handle. Just to clarify...make sure those are on there too!

Have a Call to Action

Believe it or not, sometimes people enjoy being told what to do (my preteen and teenage kids are an exception). This can also take the pressure off that awkward "so...what's next" follow up time after a conference. Literally tell those who take your card how to follow up with you . Your card could say something like "Let's hang out!" or "You seem cool. Let's be friends." And direct them to one specific, preferred way to do so (i.e. follow you on Facebook). You could even direct them to a unique url with a cool video of you talking about how excited you are to connect with them.

Focus on Collecting

This one is actually pretty unintuitive. Remember when we were kids and we collected trading cards (Garbage Pail Kids were the bomb)? Well, instead of worrying about how many business cards to bring and your goals for how many you want to hand out, set an intention to collect quality cards/contacts. This way, you control what happens afterward. On occasion, I've been so obsessed with handing out my cards that I forget to ask (or suddenly get too shy to ask) for that person's card in return. When this happens, I lose control over the follow up process and the possibilities for collaborations and partnerships. Collecting = control.

Now onto the digital aspects of your brand's identity, and there are quite a few. Your website or your brand's home is the most important piece. Now a days if you don't have a website, you don't exist. They have been saying that for years, but it becomes more and more true everyday. With the plethora (this is the last time I promise) of low-cost to no-cost online resources out there, anyone can have a website in no time. So you have no excuse!

Your social media platforms must also be well branded to reflect the value you offer. In all cases, you will need to start with a great set of photos to choose from. Think far beyond the traditional boring headshot. Those days of the head on photo in a stuffy suite with a nondescript grayish brown background are over! Instead of getting headshots, consider the concept of "habitat shots". These are beautiful pictures of you in your element and natural habitat – your home office, local coffee shop, your studio, in a park, etc. Get some shots doing what you love!

Creating a consistent digital presence through social media is key and is easy with a bit of planning.

Again, with the features and accessibility of digital resources changing daily, visit www.oliviaomega.com/breautifullybranded for more specifics around creating your digital footprint and a list of resources that I love and adore!

"Dress shabbily and they remember the dress; dress impeccably and they remember the woman."
- Coco Chanel

"You're Never Fully Dressed Without a Smile"
by Sia

Are there 3 small things that I can do daily to up my style game? Does the look of my style and brand match my value?

Chapter Thirteen

Your Balls

Every Entrepreneur Has A Pair

I keep waiting to
meet a man that
has more balls
than I do.
- Salma Hayek

Your Balls

I just had to do it! I had to mention this part of anatomy that science would prove that we don't have but I would beg to differ. Yes, you have balls! In addition to all of the parts of your brand's anatomy that we've already talked about, it takes some pretty massive-sized cojones to not only realize that you have a unique value proposition to offer people, but to also package it up and sell it in the marketplace.

Becoming an entrepreneur takes courage and bravery unlike anything else I've known.

Even if you are just starting to kick around some ideas about starting a business or creating your personal brand, you've taken a step that some only think about. It takes a lot of guts to put yourself out there, open and vulnerable for the entire world (internet and beyond) to see and potentially criticize. You are an example for women everywhere in any field. Congratulations and I commend you!

"Owning our story and loving ourselves through that process is the bravest things that we'll ever do."

- Brené Brown

What do I fear when it comes to growing my brand? How can I overcome them and what supports can I put in place to help?

Chapter Fourteen

Evolution

Constant State of Beta

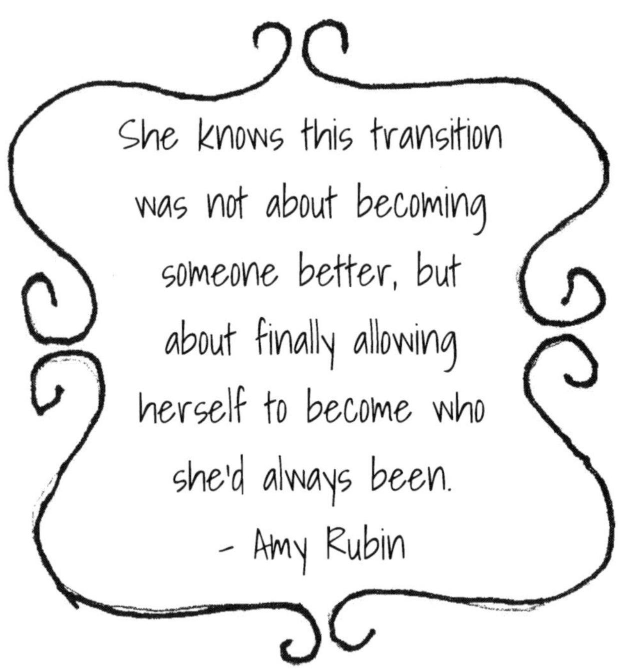
She knows this transition
was not about becoming
someone better, but
about finally allowing
herself to become who
she'd always been.
- Amy Rubin

Brand Evolution

Just as you are a woman that is changing and evolving day by day and year by year, your brand will also evolve. Women are like wine right? We just get better with time. So overtime, it's important to continue to evaluate your brand's values, direction and overall effectiveness. When launched my children's clothing line in 2007, I was in the midst of motherhood with two babies. The business I launched was perfect for the stage of life I was in. Years later, I can say that my life doesn't fit into the baby world anymore, but ultimately, my WHY has remained the same. It's just achieved and executed differently.

I urge you to continue to grow, breathe, flow and remaining flexible and open to change. With this advice I also offer a word of caution – don't be tossed left and right by every little thing that comes your way or every opinion of your friends and family. Refer back to your core focus, your brand umbrella and most importantly trust your gut in all your do. Surround yourself with people who will support your brand and who will remind you of who you are if you happen to forget in fear.

"Life is unpredictable, it changes with the season, even your coldest winter, happens for the best of reasons. And though it feels eternal, like all you'll ever do is freeze, I promise spring is coming, and with it, brand new leaves."

- Erin Hanson

"Fly"

by Nicki Minaj

How have my life stages made an impact on who I am? What are some ways I can stay grounded yet open to change?

Notes & Doodles... 

Notes & Doodles...

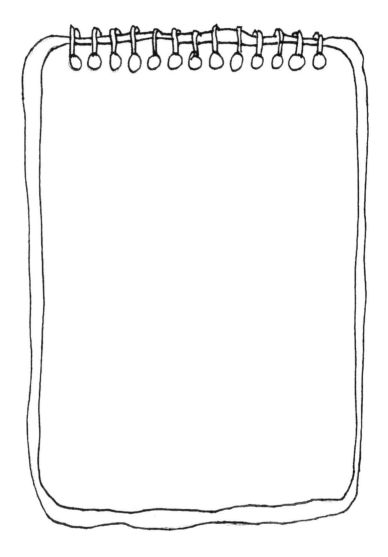

Notes & Doodles...

Notes & Doodles... 

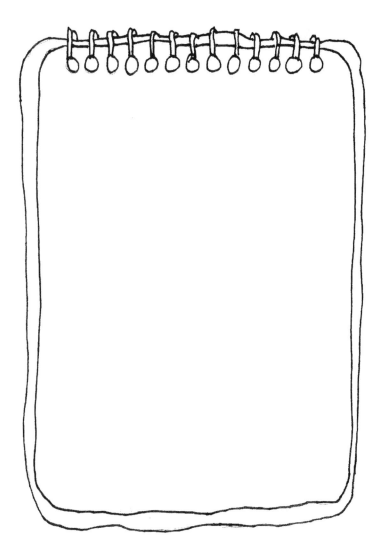

Notes & Doodles... 

Notes & Doodles... 

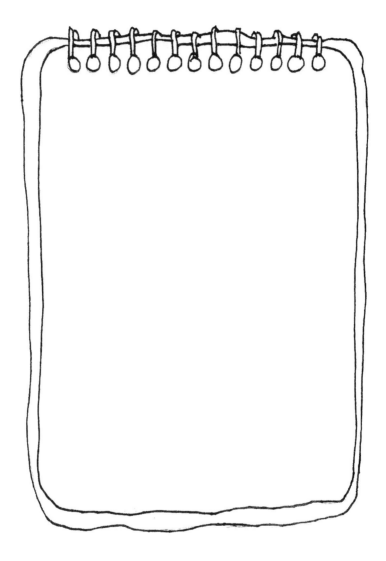

Notes & Doodles... 

Notes & Doodles...

Notes & Doodles...

About the Author

Olivia Omega is a personal branding expert, freelance consultant and speaker focused on building entrepreneurial brands. Inspiring women entrepreneurs is her passion. Through workshops, mentorship, online courses and one-on-one consultations, Olivia provide the tools needed to successfully build a heart-centered personal brand both online and offline. She is especially fond of taking smartly developed strategy and using it to develop outward-facing marketing materials and beautiful websites.

Her personal mission is to encourage creative women to walk in their God-given entrepreneurial purpose by empowering them to create an authentically unique brand…from strategy to execution and through messaging, identity and branded online experiences.

Olivia graduated with a business marketing degree from the University of Colorado at Boulder, Leeds School of Business and currently lives in Denver, CO.

Visit www.oliviaomega.com/beautifullybranded for worksheets and resources that accompany this book.

Made in the USA
Columbia, SC
14 February 2024

31556866R00085